GIRL TALK:
TRUTH EVERY WOMAN WANTS TO KNOW

Kenya M. Ransey

Table of Contents

Section I

Thesis Statement...1
Introduction 3

What is the Fear of Loneliness? 11
Why Do We Fall Prey to the Feeling of Loneliness?.........17
What Happens When You Believe a Lie?..................21

What is the Power of Being Alone? 27
Why Do We Resist "Okay Either Way"? 31
What Happens When You Embrace Singleness? 37

Section II

The Effects of Each Approach on Your Time.............45
The Effects of Each Approach on Your Money 49
The Effects of Each Approach on Your Relationships......53
Summary 57

Section III

Next Steps..61
About the Author......................................63
Acknowledgments.....................................65

Thesis Statement

This book is for women who are unmarried and ready to experience the love and companionship they desire, yet who are fearful that they will never get married or find their life partner.

This book will show you how understanding one simple distinction – the distinction between operating from the fear of being lonely versus embracing the power of being alone - is the key to attracting more of what you want in your life.

This book will show you how embracing the power of being alone empowers you to create and attract more of what you desire in three major life areas: time, money, and relationships.

Introduction

"When are you gonna get married?"

"I thought you'd be married by now..."

"Girrrl, you're getting older...don't you think it's time you settle down and get married? What are you waiting for?"

"I just don't understand...I mean, everybody wants to be happy...don't you want a man to make you happy?"

Yes. These words have actually been spoken aloud. By others. To me.

I can't tell you how many times well-intentioned people have made these and other inappropriate comments about my marital status. Chances are though, if you are reading this book, you are a woman who is familiar with these types of encounters.

Even as a young girl, I was conditioned to begin preparing for what many seem to believe is the ultimate moment of a woman's life - the day I say, "I do".

I remember so clearly, one Christmas morning, (I was around five or six years old at the time), while thoroughly enjoying the gifts I received, hearing my father question my mother about why she did not buy me any baby dolls or Barbie dolls for Christmas. I also heard him, albeit from a place of sincere concern, question my normalcy when she advised him I didn't seem to be "into dolls". I had never asked for them, spoke of them, or even played with the ones other people had given me as gifts. She informed my dad that I liked books, puzzles, and the type of toys and games that made me think and figure out things.

At this time, my parents noticed I was listening, so the conversation ended. Perhaps it resumed at another time, in my absence, of course, because at the next gift-giving occasion, I received Barbie dolls and a multi-level dollhouse mansion for the Barbies, hand-built by none other than- you guessed it - my father. I squealed with glee when I saw it. Perhaps I was excited by the sheer size of the thing (it looked much bigger than the ones advertised on television). The fact that my dad built it just for me contributed to my excitement as well. Although sincere, my excitement was fleeting. I remember playing with the Barbies and the house only once – the day I received them. In fact, the last vivid memory I have is overhearing my mother give my father an "I told you so" about the entire situation... after which, **no one** ever mentioned or purchased dolls of any kind for me ever again.

This is my first memory of social constructs and societal norms being introduced to me in an attempt to influence my expression of what it meant to be a female. The message was strong; and as time went on, it was repeated over and over and over again.

It was not my father's intention to try to make me act a certain way. Based on his experiences, girls played with dolls. His sisters played with dolls when they were younger, their daughters (my cousins) played with dolls, so he thought he should see his little girl play with dolls, too. I have always been a bit different, though. The typical things just didn't seem to interest me. In an effort to please my dad, I tried to conform, but like everything inauthentic, it just didn't last. He saw my true feelings with the dollhouse he made for me, and he resolved to just let me be myself.

This experience is just one example of what we all have encountered when we step outside the confines of other peoples' expectations for how women should behave. Hopefully, those in your life are like my parents, and they encourage and support you to be true to yourself when expressing who you are.

Throughout time, women have been inundated with countless messages and images depicting society's standard for women; even as little girls, we are shown our proverbial "place". For centuries, womanhood has been defined *for us*, not by us or even along with us. As a result, our identity and value in the world has been defined primarily by two roles: wife and mother. While both of these roles are exceptional and honorable work, they are by no means the totality of a woman's value, ability, or potential.

Even with all of the talent and savvy women possess, despite the amount of progress made in the last century and recent decades, many of us are longing inwardly for that which seems to elude us – love. So much so, that it's a commonality among women of different racial and ethnic backgrounds, varying religions and spiritual beliefs, diverse educational levels, different sexual orientations, and across all career fields. No matter the background, no matter the story, we desire love within the dynamic of an intimate relationship.

In fact, the desire is so strong, many women associate **not** being in a relationship with not being special, with being unattractive, undesirable, and incomplete. Somehow, in many of our minds, being married is equated with being an important person of value, and being unmarried or unattached is synonymous with loneliness, being broken (like something is wrong), and feeling unimportant. What makes women with great accomplishments, who live a good life (by society's standards), feel this way about themselves?

I surveyed over one hundred unmarried women I know, and what I found was staggering. Of all of the women surveyed:

- 90% described themselves as unhappy and wanting change in one or more major life areas (finances, fitness/health, and family and relationship status).
- Of those that wanted change, 100% desired marriage or a committed relationship. (84% wanted to be married, 16% didn't require marriage, but did want a committed relationship.)
- Of all of the women surveyed, only one woman…yes, just one…had no desire for marriage or a committed relationship at all (due to a previous marital experience).

The desire for love is very real, y'all. It's also good, healthy, and natural. There is absolutely nothing wrong with wanting love and marriage; yet, there is a red flag waving. My concern is about the link many of us have formed between being unmarried and unattached with being undesirable, as if marriage is a status symbol. It's as if there's a "Your Best Life" checklist, and having a husband is the final box we need to check off before we can hold up our list and prove to the world that we're okay. The truth is that those who are married are no better than nor superior to those of us who are not. So, if we have attached our worth as a woman to being married, then we must look closely at what we believe about unmarried women and how that causes us to see ourselves.

In this book, we will take a close look at some common misconceptions that we have been conditioned to believe are true about unmarried women. We will also look at alternatives to those thoughts and beliefs, so that we can make an informed decision about what we ultimately choose to believe. According to Sharon Hughes, *What Happens When You Believe*, "It is what we believe that shapes our lives.". Our beliefs determine our daily choices, and our quality of life is nothing more than the decisions we make over time. Most of us make what we think are good choices based on the information we are given; at the same time...when you know better, you do better.

This is in no way a slight toward anyone or the decisions they have made in the past. This is merely an acknowledgment that life is full of experiences, and from those experiences we have two choices: live and learn, or live and relive. Hopefully, we all live and learn. Those who are wise make an effort to learn continuously throughout life. I hope this describes you. I hope that you are reading this book with an open mind, that you are ready to consider what is set before you, and that you utilize what is applicable in ways that encourage you to learn and grow.

Currently, I walk through life as a confident, self-assured, unmarried woman, but I haven't always been this way. It was in my journey to becoming who I am now that I realized how I had been sold a bill of goods through the years. I heard and accepted misinformation that needed correcting if I was to be my best self and to live my best life every single day.

If you think there's even a slight chance that this describes you, too...keep reading! If you think that maybe, just maybe, somewhere along your path in life you were given misinformation, accepted a wrong message, or perhaps are missing a piece of the big puzzle...keep reading! If you know in your heart, that there is more to life than what you are experiencing now, and that you want and were made for more...keep reading! In this text are tools to equip and empower you with what you need to properly address your desire to be loved. It may take a little work, but it's nothing you can't handle! So, if you are as ready and as excited as I am, let's begin! Our journey awaits!

What is the Fear of Loneliness?

Simply stated, the fear of loneliness is the worry and extreme concern that you are not (nor will you ever be) loved, supported, and valued. It is the fear that you won't experience "belonging to someone of your own", and that if you do not experience love through the dynamic of a committed relationship, then

- You are of little worth and value.
- You are not enough.
- You are incomplete and unloved.
- Your inherent need to give and receive love will go unnoticed - or even worse - it might be seen but flat-out denied.

Deep within, we all have the need for love. Regardless of our gender, race, ethnicity, religion or spiritual beliefs, sexual orientation, or socioeconomic status, we all desire the same thing(s) - to be loved and valued. Not only is this a longing desire, I believe it is a right. We all deserve to be in loving relationships with honor and respect as the foundation of our interactions.

To be loved and valued is a desire we all have. Everybody wants to be loved. Not only does everyone want to be loved, but everyone *needs* it. So, if we have this need to be loved and we have a desire for love (marriage/committed relationship), they must go hand-in-hand, right? Well, not exactly.

To be honest, a romantic relationship is not the only way your need for love can be met. In fact, a person's need for love can and *should* be met in a variety of ways and through a number of relationships. Marriage should not be anyone's only source of receiving love and feeling valued. Yes, it most definitely should enhance your life, but the very source of your life...it should not be!

I am not saying that you shouldn't want to be married. I'm not knocking marriage or the desire to marry. I believe I would like to be married one day. That's not the issue, so let's look beyond the desire. Okay - so you want to be married, but it hasn't happened yet. Not only hasn't it happened, but there may be no viable prospects on the horizon or even in your periphery...annnnd time is passing you by. So, what now? Are you worried? Are you scared? Losing hope? If yes, why? Why are you worried? Why are you scared? Why do you feel discouraged? These feelings are all a result of the fear of loneliness.

Webster defines **loneliness** as "sadness due to not having friends or companions". Other related words are isolation, isolated, abandoned, abandonment, unloved, unwanted, rejected, rejection, and outcast.

Loneliness is an emotion which comes from being or feeling isolated and without support, as if there is nothing and no one like you, with you, or in your corner. Loneliness has nothing to do with marital status because some of the loneliest people are currently married or in relationships. Being physically alone or unattached is not the cause of loneliness. Loneliness goes beyond bodily presence. It goes beyond anything physical because people experience loneliness even when others are around.

According to this interpretation of loneliness, most unmarried women are not lonely. What I'm saying is, most unmarried women are not abandoned outcasts. Most are not friendless. On the contrary, most have a life full of acquaintances and companions. Some have so many, they classify who they know into groups based on various interests, similarities, and commonalities. Take a look at your own life and the lives of some unmarried women you know. For the most part, they engage in loving relationships and have a support system which consists of family, friends, and a tried-and-true, "ride-or-die" crew they can depend on whenever needed.

Does this describe you? If so, then what you feel is not actually loneliness. We've defined loneliness, and that is not really what you're experiencing. You are feeling what I call the *fear of loneliness*, and it is a reality in many peoples' lives. It's not actual loneliness, it is **fear that you will be lonely and experience loneliness** (as defined by Webster), **if you do not get married**. It stems from the belief that marriage is a woman's sole and primary source of love, worth, value, and companionship; and, that without marriage, you are an isolated, abandoned, unloved, unwanted, rejected outcast.

The fear of loneliness occurs from giving marriage (or being married) a value *above* all else, including the value you have for yourself. In this belief system, you think that being married makes you more valuable than you are alone or unmarried. In essence, you see yourself as a lesser person solely because you are not married. You believe that you don't measure up, that you alone are not enough, and that marriage will make you more valued, more respected, and more accepted.

This feeling outweighs everything else. So, regardless of what you may have present in your life: dream job, successful business, strong support system, loving family, good friends, the "finer things in life", etc., you wrestle with a feeling of inadequacy because this one area in your life is not how you think it should be. Becoming a wife trumps all! You are afraid you may never get married because, somewhere within, you believe that you need consent from someone other than yourself to be whole and secure in who you are, and you are looking to marriage to create feelings of acceptance, approval, and validation.

There's a common saying in which fear is an acronym that describes itself - **F**alse **E**vidence **A**ppearing **R**eal, and that is what applies here. The fear of loneliness (FOL) is a smokescreen. It is deception rooted in misconceptions, misinformation, and displaced expectations about love, our need for love, and how that need should be addressed. Ultimately, it is a distraction. It inhibits us from seeing what is actually before us, and it keeps us from what we really want.

Why Do We Fall Prey to the Feeling of Loneliness?

If you have fallen prey to the fear of loneliness, it is because of one reason: you were told a lie; and at some point, you believed it. When we hear something over and over, it's usually just a matter of time before we accept it and believe it to be true.

For the majority of our lives, mass media has been used over and over, in a variety of ways, to relay one overarching message. A message I refer to as **The Big Lie**.

The Big Lie

Marriage is the ultimate achievement to be attained in a woman's life because she, on her own, is not enough; furthermore, no amount of personal and/or professional accomplishments measure up to "landing" a man and getting married. A woman's needs for love, value, and self-worth are only met when she becomes a wife.... all else is insufficient.

The Big Lie has been communicated to us over and over throughout time and across various social constructs (relationships, mass media, religion). After a while, it's only natural that we accept it and believe it to be the truth. Buying into **The Big Lie** is why a woman can have a great career with meaningful work, a loving support system with a myriad of healthy relationships, a substantial salary, a nice home, a fancy car, and all of the other factors of a "good life"; and yet, within her heart, she can still feel unhappy, sad, and discontent. It's why, in spite of living a life FULL of tremendous blessings and abundance in all other areas, we can believe we are still not experiencing the truest form of happiness because this one event has not occurred in our lives by the time we expected it to happen.

Another Lie

How many of you realize that what starts as one lie never stops with just one lie? Whenever a lie is told, it's just a matter of time before additional lies must be told in order to maintain and uphold the main lie (**The Big Lie**). The sacrament of marriage is no exception. In our case, ladies, **The Big Lie** has been further perpetuated by a supplemental lie that you have probably believed as well, and that is the notion that **getting married is the source and key to living happily ever after.** Life for an unattached woman is unable to be thoroughly enjoyed until a man decides to show up and save her from the dismal conditions of her life (whatever they may be). (I seriously laugh at the thought of this every time.)

Now, before some of you get all riled up, please understand that this is **not** a male-bashing session, nor an attack on the value of having good men in your life. Good men are indeed valuable and they are capable of contributing to our lives in meaningful ways. What this is, is a flat-out refusal of the following notions:

- A woman is in need of a man to obtain value. Her sense of self-worth on its own is not enough.
- An unmarried woman is of less value than a married woman.
- Being someone's wife will make you more than you are as an unmarried woman.
- Marriage is the key to a happy life.

These are the messages that have been presented to us over time; and in the absence of an alternative, it's no wonder that at some point, most of us believed it even though it couldn't be any further from the truth. So, what happens when what we believe to be true is actually a lie? Let's look at how this has affected us.

What Happens When You Believe a Lie?

The Cost of This Approach

What we believe shapes our lives. It doesn't matter if what we believe is true or false because the power is not in what is presented to us but in what we *believe*.

Your life is shaped by what you believe. This means that what you accept as truth becomes a reality in your world...it becomes your experience... whether or not it is actually true.

Let me tell you a story to help explain what I mean.

I remember a time when I wanted to lose weight. I was in overdrive, doing way more than the minimum program requirements, but no matter what I tried, I just wasn't seeing results. Naturally, after some time, I began to get discouraged.

"See…I knew it…," I said. "I can't lose weight no matter what I do or how hard I try."

It was this expression of frustration which took me on a journey that helped me discover what I truly believed about myself, and how what I accepted as truth was keeping me from losing weight. Long before I started the workout regimen, I "bought into" the idea that no matter what I did, I would never be successful in reaching my weight loss goal. I actually told myself that since I didn't come from "a skinny family" (neither side is skinny, y'all), I just needed to *accept* the fact that I would always fight a losing battle when it came to managing my weight. I mean, I wanted to lose weight so badly, at times it drove me to tears. I did the work on the outside, but all the while, deep in my heart, I held beliefs that simply were not true, and those beliefs were hindering my progress.

So, although what I told myself wasn't actually factual or true in reality, the moment I accepted it as truth and believed it to be true, it *became* true for me - it became my experience. To undo the effects of this, I first had to acknowledge that what I believed and accepted as truth was really a lie! When I replaced the lies with actual truths, I was able to focus on what I wanted to manifest in my life and become successful in my weight loss efforts.

Belief empowers reality. If you have accepted **The Big Lie's** message as truth, and if you believe that you are in need of a relationship or a spouse to attain value and to create a feeling of self-worth, then your beliefs will manifest these thoughts as your reality. So, regardless of your abilities, all the good in your life, and all of the value you add to the world just by being you, that won't be enough for you. You won't be content or enjoy your life to the fullest because what you believe is rooted in inadequacy and putting negative energy into the world. What you give out is what is attracted back to you, and it becomes your life experience.

When You Believe a Lie, You Attract What You Do Not Want

The Big Lie is detrimental because it causes us to only focus on the things we don't have - and focus is like fertilizer - whatever you put it on grows. Focusing on what we don't have or don't want is what I call taking a **position of resistance.** Even when taking a stand *against* the things we don't want, we are giving our energy and attention to what we don't like, thereby causing negativity to grow within and around us. As long as there is resistance to the truth about what exists, you cannot create what you long for.

Focusing on what you don't have, don't like, or don't want is a source of frustration which costs you the joyful experience of living fully in the present moment. The past is gone, and the future is uncertain. The only thing we have is the present; yet, when you choose to use this approach, you are unable to fully enjoy your life as it is now. This approach is deceivng because focusing on what's missing in your life keeps you from seeing and enjoying the goodness that is already before you. A more effective approach is to focus on what you have and on the changes you desire. Being grateful for what is already present in your life is the pathway to more of what you want.

Believing a lie renders you powerless and results in feeling helpless

This is why **The Big Lie** is so dangerous. It diminishes your power and gives it to other people. It takes from you the power to choose how you see, define, and value yourself and gives it to people and things outside of you. **The Big Lie** allows other people to define you and assign you a value based on their thoughts, ideas, perceptions, values, hang-ups, insecurities, and beliefs.

Believing **The Big Lie** strips you of your power to choose how to demonstrate and display femininity and womanhood in the distinct exquisiteness of your individuality. Believing the lies means you trade the privilege to authentically express all of you - your gifts, your talents, your skills and abilities, for what "they" think and what "they" say. This is bondage because you are held captive by others' opinions about who you are, how you should act, what you should do, and how they would live your life if they were you.

Believing a Lie Results in Fear

Another result of believing a lie is fear. Knowing (here knowing means believing) the truth is what makes us free (John 8:32); so, if believing the truth brings freedom, then believing a lie does the opposite. It brings fear which is bondage. Fear is bondage since it causes us to freeze or get "stuck", and it hinders or even halts any progress in our lives.

Your power is in what you believe. Whether it's true or untrue, your acceptance is the power which sets things in motion to manifest your beliefs in your life.

If what you are believing is actual truth, then what will manifest as a result is freedom, life, and authenticity.

Fear, constraints, bondage, and resistance are the results of accepting a lie as truth and believing it. The good news in all of this is that if you have been believing a lie, you can stop! And once you stop, the untruth loses its power and can no longer hold you back or keep you stuck in a place where you don't want to be.

The thing about fear is that it only possesses the power we give to it. The way to deal with fear is to expose it for what it is. You don't have to blab everything to the whole world. The key is to expose it in honesty, even if it's just to yourself. Just as I did with my beliefs about weight loss, you must first acknowledge that what you previously believed and accepted as reality was really a lie, and then replace those falsehoods with actual truth, so that you will be free to focus on exactly what you want manifested in your life.

What is the Power of Being Alone?

Let's start with the meaning of the word ***alone***. This word is commonly interchanged and associated with the word lonely, when in fact, the two words couldn't be more different. So that we are all clear on what's being communicated, let's look at the definitions.

According to Webster, and for all intents and purposes of this book, the word ***alone*** means:

- Having no one else present (at the moment).
- On one's own.
- Without others' help or participation.

lonely vs. alone

lonely	alone
- isolated - friendless - abandoned - unloved - unwanted - rejected - outcast	- having no one else present (at the moment) - on one's own - without others' help or participation

There may be a connection in our minds between these two words, but they have completely different meanings.

Standing in the Power of Being Alone is to stand in the authority of who you are, as you are *on your own*...to be in a healthy, loving, relationship with yourself and to know you have value simply because you know who you are. To stand in the Power of Being Alone (PBA) is to know you have value because you are you and not solely because of the role(s) that you fill for others (wife, mother, friend, etc.).

Standing in PBA means you know and believe that nothing and no one outside of you can increase your value as a human being because you are as valuable now as you ever will be. Your value will never increase or decrease because of what you have or don't have, do or don't do...including getting married. When you stand in

PBA, you know that if all external characteristics and factors about you were to change tomorrow, you would still know who you are, and have *a clear, undeniable, and unwavering awareness of your value and sense of self-worth.*

Standing in PBA means you are aware of your worth and value, without others' help or participation and regardless of anyone else's opinion. When you stand in the Power of Being Alone, it doesn't mean that you don't want loving relationships in your life. You wholeheartedly welcome and embrace those who want to love and support you. However, should someone decide not to "join your team" or partner with you, it shouldn't cause you to question your worth. When you stand in the power of being alone, it causes you to be what I like to call "okay either way". This means you refuse to give into the fear of loneliness, and you do not settle for less than you deserve just for the sake of having somebody in your life. "Okay either way" is the attitude that although being in a committed relationship is a very real desire, the standard for your relationships is that others honor, respect, support, and value you. This, in fact, is a ***requirement*** because being in a relationship is not more important than your dignity and self-respect.

Adopting the "okay either way" position means you love, value, and respect yourself enough to enjoy and make the most of your life...whether married or unmarried. Knowing your marital/relationship status doesn't affect the core of who you are; you embrace who you are and what you bring to the table *before* anyone enters your life, and you remain just as aware of this, should the person exit your life. When you stand in the power of being alone, it means you possess a healthy self-image, a true picture of who you are on your own. As a result, you only engage in mutually-beneficial relationships where all parties give and receive in a healthy, balanced exchange.

Why Do We Resist "Okay Either Way"?
(The Underlying Dynamic at Play)

SO! If standing in the power of being alone is one of authority and choice, why do we resist? Why don't we embrace being "okay either way"? Where's the disconnect between our heads (what we know) and our hearts (how we feel)?

Tough truth: We resist "okay either way" because we are not single. The word single does not mean unmarried. Unmarried is a term that describes your relationship or marital status. Single, on the other hand, is something altogether different.

Let me explain it this way:

Another way I like to say 'standing in the power of being alone' is standing in or "embracing singleness". Unfortunately, in our society, the word **single** has been dumbed-down in its meaning, and it has become an ugly, "four-letter word". To help change your perception of the word, I want you to think of a one-dollar bill; you know, a "single". Picture it just out in the open somewhere. No one else is around, so it doesn't belong to anybody. When you come across this "single", would you think, "Oh, it's alone, so it is undesirable and has no value. It's not worth anything by itself, so I'll just leave it here until it finds another dollar bill willing to partner with it before I pick it up?"

Of course not. No one would react that way! When we study this closely, we realize that each and every one-dollar bill manufactured is separate, unique, and whole. That each "single" has a set value, and can stand on its own. It does not need to be accompanied by another dollar bill to have value, and when it is with other bills, that doesn't add to its worth at all. Its value remains the same as it was when it was alone. Regardless of who sees the dollar bill, who overlooks it, whether it is by itself, or with others like it, it is what it is, and the same is true for you. You also have a manufacturer who took great time to craft you as you are, making **you** separate, unique, and whole. You, too, can stand on your own. Regardless of who recognizes your worth (or not), and despite what some of your life experiences may tell you, your value is what it is. You are exceptional... your identity and value are unique...and this will never, ever change!

When we truly accept and believe this to be true, we embrace singleness, and when we embrace singleness, we become okay either way. When you know who you are, you are not willing to accept less than what you deserve, even if that means remaining alone. It doesn't matter what others think or what society says because you are self-aware, you are comfortable with yourself, and you are secure in what you expect. You have your own standards.

Unfortunately, those who lack a solid understanding of themselves look for other people's approval and opinions to define who they are. What other people think takes priority because they have not taken the time to discover their own heart, mind, and desires. As a result, they are not "okay either way", and they are not single, they are simply unmarried.

In many ways, the Fear of Loneliness and The Power of Being Alone are antithetical. They are polar opposites, and we are believing and operating our lives from either one place or the other. "Is it really that definite?" you may ask. Yes... it really is!

According to Dr. Helen Schuchmann, *A Course in Miracles*, "There are no harmless or neutral thoughts." Our thoughts are the source of our creative energy, and "they produce [within us] either peace and love, or war and fear." So, when it comes to our thought life, it's black and white...there is no gray area. And if we are honest with ourselves, *we can look at our lives to see the path of our thought life and what we believe*. What do your thoughts produce within you? Are you living your dreams or your fears?

As we've said before, what we focus on grows. The things on which we put our attention are magnified, both in our minds and in our experiences. What you believe shapes your life. Another way to say this is when you focus on what you don't want, you give energy (which is life) to your fears and cause them to appear in your life. We give our energy and focus to things in three ways:

- Mentally through our thoughts.
- Physically through our actions and the motivation or the why behind them.
- Verbally through the words we speak.

Energy is always in motion, and our energy (what we think, say, and do) moves us in one of two directions - either toward or away from what it is we want in our lives. It simply is not possible to operate our lives from a place of fear and expect to experience freedom and joy. We cannot operate with a mindset of lack and expect to experience abundance and wealth. **We attract more of what we want in our lives by focusing on what it is we want to see happen, not on what we don't want.**

Women who are "okay either way" are not in a position of resistance. Yes, they desire marriage, and although that is not their current reality, they are not resistant to the reality of being unmarried. Their focus is not on what they don't have, don't want, or don't like in their life. They are "okay either way" because they are making the most of the present. To the degree that they can, they are creating the life they desire to live, and they are enjoying it fully.

Those who believe **The Big Lie** live in fear, and fear keeps us frozen. It causes us to operate from a place of what we don't want; thereby, causing us to attract more of what we despise and want to eliminate from our lives. When we don't want something (For example, I don't want to be single.), we are in resistance to that thought. Operating from a place of resistance will only produce negative results. Referring back to my example, my unsuccessful weight loss attempts revolved around a struggle with my then reality of not wanting to be overweight. My focus was on what I *didn't want to happen*, and it caused me to be unsuccessful. My focus grew and was attracted to me, making my experience the very thing I did not want. As long as I was focused on what I did not want, what I did not want was my experience.

We can not create what we want by operating from a place of resistance. The key here, and the key to being "okay either way", is to drop your battle with your believed reality, and embrace where you currently are in life. Once I let go of what I didn't want, acknowledged the reality of where I was, declared where I wanted to be, and made a plan to get there, it made quite the difference...I saw results!

Even if where you are right now is not at all what you desire or how you imagined your life would be at this stage, it's where you are, so embrace it and all of what it entails. Be thankful for where you are and what you have **now**. Acknowledge and accept it so you can become unstuck, and then focus on what you do want. By doing this, you allow yourself to enter into a powerful place of attraction to your desires.

What Happens When You Embrace Singleness?

Standing in the power of being alone provides empowerment.

The benefit of this approach is the move from a place of fear, loneliness, and uncertainty (because of your marital status) to one of empowerment and security in who you truly are.

Our life and the quality of our life is nothing more than the sum total of the decisions we make over time. No matter what, **we always have a choice.** We make choices every day. The benefit of standing in the power of being alone is that you are choosing to move through life not as a victim, but as the victor; not as one who is powerless, but as one who is empowered. Although you may not like your current situation (marital status), the truth is you are *not* powerless when it comes to your life. What you experience is up to you because ultimately, you have the power of choice.

Standing in the power of being alone inspires you and supplies you with the courage to go after what it is you want. Because of this power, when you stand in PBA, you choose to take life by the horns. You accept the responsibility of creating the life you long for. It is my belief that we are created beings. Whether you use the name God, The Creator, Life Source, Energy, The Universe, or something else, She/He (I'm not going to participate in the gender debate either) is the source of everything. I believe that there is a Master Creator, and a small part of The Creator is in all of us. This, by default, makes us creators as well. Creative power is within you, so *you* have the authority and the ability to bring about the life you desire. We all possess the capability to create, and no one is more responsible for your life than you. Embracing the power of being alone takes you from sideline spectator to active participant in the game of life; where you can determine what you want to happen...and see it through.

If you are willing to stand in PBA and embrace singleness by making the most of your life where you are now, then you **CAN** have what it is you really want. I say this with confidence because I am looking beyond the surface, at the real issue. There is nothing wrong with the desire for marriage, companionship, etc. What you really want is to live your life unafraid and to improve your quality of life by making decisions and operating from a place of freedom and empowerment rather than loneliness and fear. Perhaps you think the feeling of loneliness will go away when someone is in your life, but that's not guaranteed...in fact, some of the loneliest people in the world are married.

What is guaranteed is that releasing your fear and adopting a position of security and empowerment, even though you are alone, will start the process of attracting and manifesting what's right for you. You are already okay just as you are now. **You** just have to **believe** it, **and act** upon it!

Okay...you want a life partner. I get that, but what are you doing with your life in the meantime?

The most important relationship you will ever develop is the one you have with yourself because it is the foundation for how you relate to the people and things in your life. Are you living or are you letting life pass you by? Are you waiting for someone to show up to tell you to go after your dreams and desires? And what if no one shows up? Is all of the happiness in your life contained within the decisions and choices of another person? Not so when you stand in the power of being alone. Embracing your singleness provides you with freedom of choice and the ability to see things through. The ball is in your court, so take your best shot!

What Standing in the Power of Being Alone is NOT

Standing in the power of being alone is not an anti-marriage position. It is not predicated on the belief that you are weak if you desire to be a wife or to be in a committed, loving relationship. It is perfectly okay, normal, and healthy to embrace singleness and to simultaneously desire marriage. They are not mutually exclusive, so you're not required to choose one or the other. You can be one and desire the other at the same time!

Another misnomer is that those who stand in the power of being alone do so because they have adopted the belief that they do not want or need anyone, and they would rather go through life not allowing other people to get too close or become too involved. This is not standing in the power of being alone. This is a guarded approach that is rooted in unresolved hurt and disappointment. Operating out of pain does not yield beneficial results. On the contrary, standing in the power of being alone allows us to be comfortable in vulnerability with others because when we're okay with who we are as we are, it is wisdom (not our desires) which determines the level of trust we assign to others and how soon we do this.

Recap

Let's review what we've covered so far:

We've discussed two approaches to life as an unmarried/unattached woman:

The Fear of Loneliness (FOL) vs. Standing in PBA

Key Terms	**Lonely** - isolated, friendless, abandoned, unloved, unwanted, rejected, outcast	**Alone** - having no one else present (at the moment), on one's own, without others' help or participation. Another word for **alone** is single which means separate, unique, and whole.
What is it?	Extreme concern, worry, and fear that stems from the belief that you will live a lonely life if you never marry	To stand in the authority of who you are, to love, accept, and value yourself as you are on your own, without any input, help, or participation from others

Underlying Dynamic	The belief that: Marriage is the source of love, worth, value, and a happy life (happily ever after) You cannot be truly or fully happy unless/until you are married because as an unmarried woman, you are an isolated, abandoned, unloved, unwanted, rejected, an outcast.	The belief that: You are already as valuable right now - in this moment - as you will ever be; that no one and no thing can add or take away any value to who you are as a person. It (marriage) can add tremendous value to your life experience but not to you as a person. Remember to reference the one-dollar bill – "the single". Knowing and understanding that the most important relationship you will ever have is with yourself because it is the basis for how you relate to all else.

	Feeling Powerless	Empowerment
The Results of this Approach	Evaluating yourself according to others' standards and expectations which surrenders the power for defining who you are. **Fear** Fear is due to not having control of a situation. You want something in your life to be different. If you could change it, you would have done so by now. So, you feel you have no control over the situation, and you don't know what you can do about it. The result of this loss of control is fear. **Resistance** leads to *attracting more of what you DON'T want*	Take back your ability to choose how you define yourself, who you are, and the type of life you want to live. **Courage** Courage to make things happen by going after what you want. **Full acceptance and gratitude of the present moment** which opens the door to *attract and receive more of what you want.*

Other Important Truths:

- The power is not in what is presented to us as truth, but in what we believe.
- We choose what to believe.
- You can change your life by simply changing what you believe.

~~~~~~~~~~~~~~~~~~~~~~~~~~~

Hopefully, Standing in the Power of Being Alone is the approach you want to take in your life moving forward. Now that you're willing to take the leap, I'm going to lay out how making this one distinction has the power to change your time, money, and relationships.

The Effects of Each Approach on Your Time

- **Time is unwavering.** It passes continuously...always moving forward...time does not rewind or stop.

- **Time is unforgiving.** Time waits for no one. There is no way to "make up for lost time". Time that has been lost or wasted cannot be regained. Once it's gone, it's gone, and there is no getting it back.

- **Time is unbiased.** No amount of influence, power, money, or fame matters to time. The rules of time are the same for all of mankind, regardless of what you have, where you are from, or who you know.

- **Time is unconventional.** One thing that remains consistent throughout time is the amount of time we have in a day. We all know the amount, we are all given the same amount, and it never changes; yet, the amount of time we have in life [how many days we will have] is unknown and varies from person to person. Sure, there are things we can do that increase or lower our chances of living, but for the most part, we all are unaware of when our time on Earth will end.

- **Time is of the essence.** Time's characteristics and attributes demand that we understand just how important life is. In fact, we do ourselves a great disservice if we don't accept this fact. Time is an invaluable gift, given to us without cost; however, in a sense, it's not truly ours because it has its own conditions. We all are given time, but since we don't really know how much we are granted, the only time we truly have control over is the present moment. The one thing we are permitted to decide is how we use our time. My hope is that you spend it living a fulfilled life doing what your heart desires…anything else is merely existing.

Someone operating out of the Fear of Loneliness (FOL) expresses a lack of value and disregard for time. They are "stuck" and are constantly reliving the past, and/or putting off living for the future (when XYZ happens), all the while forsaking the power of the present by neglecting to be and to live fully in the current moment.

Someone Standing in the Power of Being Alone (PBA) values time. They treat it with honor and respect by maximizing what they have.

	Fear of Loneliness	Power of Being Alone
Position	Disrespect/disregard for time	Respects and values time
Ways this is Evident	Lives as if they are frozen in time. Either stuck in the past or paralyzed waiting for the future. Living in the Past: This is beyond reminiscing. This is refusing to let the past go and not moving forward. Awaiting Life, the Future: Waiting for X to happen in order to do Y. Allowing the plans and actions of others to dictate what you do and don't do. Not doing things you really want to do because certain	Maximizes time by living fully in the present moment and going after the things that you desire to be and to do...NOW! Not putting desires, dreams, or life on hold because you have no partner with which to share these experiences. Operates from the understanding that the amount of time on Earth is unknown; so, this person is selective about how time is spent, including to whom and to what it is given. Standing in PBA causes you to spend time in meaningful

	circumstances are not as you would like them. i.e. I am waiting until I am in a relationship to travel to Paris because it's the City of Love, and I'm not involved with anyone.	ways, even if that means spending time solo (alone), rather than in the company of others. Furthermore, you avoid giving time to futile activities and relationships just for the sake of not being by yourself.
The Cost/ Benefit of this Approach	The cost of FOL is time itself. As long as you operate from this perspective, life is passing you by.	The benefit of PBA is that you experience your best life. You live and enjoy a full life because you seize the moment and live in it fully.

"'Someday' is the disease that will cause you to take your dreams with you to the grave." - Tim Ferris

The Effects of Each Approach on Your Money

You may work hard for the money, and the choice is yours how to spend it; but like anything in life (time, energy, effort), your choice must have a focus in order to make an impact.

Tell your money where to go, or you won't know where it went.

You may have heard the saying "Pay yourself first.", in reference to finances and preparing for life beyond today. Whether you prefer saving, investing, or treating yourself to something special, the key is to honor yourself just as you honor others with the money you've earned. The position from which we operate our lives (FOL vs PBA) determines just how we choose to do this.

Fear of Loneliness – People who are living in fear see money as a definer and a key to one's relevance. They may, at times, use money to soothe their pain and/or declare to the world their value by purchasing nice things. There's nothing wrong with wanting and having nice things. Like anything else, the why behind an action like this is as important (if not more important) than the action itself. Using external adornments of any kind (possessions, titles, degrees, money, status, etc.) to define yourself (or others) is done by someone who is unsure of their identity.

Along with things such as comfort-eating and retail therapy, these are acts in which we use money to search for external solutions to an internal, intangible problem. In other words, the feeling that is attained after each purchase. Feelings like this are often-times fleeting because they do not address the root cause of the problem at hand, so the negative action is repeated over and over again.

FOL vs PBA

Position	Vision/perspective is for today. Concern is about the here and now.	Looks beyond the here and now. Sees money as a tool to be used strategically to design their desired life and to accomplish goals.
	Lives for today. Often makes finance-related decisions (purchases, quitting a job, etc.) based on how they feel at the moment, with little-to-no thought about their decision's impact on their lives or the consequences down the line. Uses money as a tool to establish one's identity, compensate for insecurities and/or shortcomings, and soothes one's intangible problems and pain.	Pays them self first - whether it be by saving, investing, or occasionally treating themselves. This is a balanced person who has a healthy relationship within them self, and it reflects in their relationship with money. Everything in moderation.

Ways this is Evident	Lacks financial goals OR May have dreams and desires but can't visualize how to reach the goal from their current reality. As a result, they accept and believe their dream is not possible for them, or it's not worth the effort or sacrifice due to obstacles they face on their journey - from where they are currently to where they want to be. If there are financial goals, there is no plan by which to achieve these goals.	

"Wealth will never open its doors to those who are unwilling to pay the price in terms of sweat, sacrifice, and hard work."
- Dennis Kimbro

The Effects of Each Approach on Your Relationships

The first and most important relationship you have is the one with yourself. It is the basis of how you relate to everyone and everything around you. How we interact with others is a mirror of how we see ourselves. The value you put on yourself is displayed in how you treat others. When you love yourself, you see in your reflection someone who is special and worthy, so you treat yourself as such.

On the contrary, when we look to others to add value to our lives, we can't see any value within ourselves. Those who respect and honor themselves have no problem giving respect and honor to others. People who dishonor and devalue their own person treat others in shameful and diminished ways. It is impossible to respect others if you lack respect for yourself… you cannot give what you do not have. What we think and how we feel about ourselves determines how we relate to and interact with others.

FOL vs PBA

Position	Lacks self-awareness, self-respect, and/or a healthy relationship with oneself.	Self-aware. Healthy respect for self and others.
	Uses others' standards and opinions to define themselves. This leads to: Comparison of self with others. Competition with others. Feelings of superiority or inferiority (as a result of the comparison & competition). Prioritizing other peoples' opinions over your own mind, heart, and desires.	Defines self and needs according to own standards. Clearly communicates boundaries and expectations to others. Respects the boundaries of others. Comfortable in their own skin, so there is no need to compare themselves with others. Appreciates others for who they are, enjoys the similarities and commonalities, and

| Ways This Is Evident | Devaluing of self and denying your own needs and expectations by accepting less than you deserve in order to please someone and/or keep them in your life.

Looks to others as their source of validation and worth.

This makes it difficult, at best, for this person to give support and love in a healthy exchange (without conditions or strings attached).

There is little-to-no sense of self, love, or value within — there is nothing for others to draw upon for support. | values differences and the uniqueness each person brings to the relationship.

Sustains a high value for self and others.

Will not accept or give less than what is deserved in a relationship (respect, honesty, trust, etc.) and will walk away from all relationships where this is not honored by everyone involved.

Looks within for source of validation and approval. All other sources of love and support are supplemental.

Able to give support and love in a healthy exchange because a healthy love for self already exists. |
|---|---|---|

"Learn to love yourself before you try to love other people. The level, degree, and quality of your singleness is the foundation of all of your relationships: personal, professional, and social." - Dr. Myles Munroe

Summary

Whether you are reflecting on time, money, or relationships... the lesson is the same:

It all begins within.

Our relationships with other people and things act as a mirror reflecting back to us how we relate to ourselves. You can only value other people and things to the degree that you value yourself.

Now that you've been made aware of these two options, the choice is yours.

If Standing in the Power of Being Alone is the approach you wish to manifest in your life, here is what it takes to accomplish your goal.

First, *decide*. It really is that simple. The choice is yours. Decide if you want change or more of the same.

Now that you have made a conscious decision, *commit to the process and to travel the road that unfolds in front of you*. When you say you want change, what you are saying is that you are willing to confront your fears and to adopt a new perspective and mindset in order to change your life. Make no mistake - this takes courage, and it is work; nevertheless, it can be achieved. You will encounter some (internal) challenges, discomfort, and awkwardness along the way, but you have to decide if what you will receive in the end is worth seeing the journey through. You have to decide that ***you*** are worth completing the process. This process will require something that is hard for many of us to do - release control. Are you willing to be "okay either way"? Are you willing to accept that you may remain unmarried...and choose to enjoy your life anyway? It may not be the end result you want; **but**, if you are not willing to accept it (show resistance), then this won't work for you. It's okay to want what you want. It is also necessary to be able to adjust and move forward if what you want doesn't happen.

If you are willing to be "okay either way", and if you are intent on living your best life - married or unmarried - then you **CAN** have what you desire. Currently, it is the fear of loneliness that keeps many of us from standing in the power of being alone. What is guaranteed is that releasing your fear and adopting a position of security and empowerment will start the process of attracting and manifesting what's right for you.

    I say this with confidence because what we all really want is to live life authentically and unafraid; to improve our quality of life by operating from a place of freedom, empowerment, and security in who we are and what we choose. People are often more comfortable with uniformity than with expressions of uniqueness, but it is only when you become comfortable being yourself that your uniqueness will shine through. It is only then that you are standing in the light of who you are, making yourself a light to others. As we embrace singleness and stand in the power of being separate, unique, and whole, it is only then that instead of longing to attach to others, we find that others are drawn to us. It becomes clear that what we once searched for *outside of ourselves* has eluded us, not because it was hiding, but because it was located deep *within us* all along.

Next Steps

Congratulations! You have reached the end of the book which means you are aware of standing in the power of being alone and what it means, and awareness is half the battle. So, what's next? Well, it is time to act. Now that you realize there is a better way to live, you are in position to experience better things, and you can start right now!

That being said, Rome was not built in a day, and neither are we. Change and development take time and practice, so while you must be willing to do the work, you also must be gentle with yourself. You won't do everything correctly the first time - none of us do. One of the great joys of life is to learn to enjoy the journey. You will never be perfect, but as long as you are honest with yourself about where you currently are, you can and will continue to make progress and to move forward.

With that in mind, something to consider is connecting with an accountability partner or personal coach during this process. (It often helps to have someone who is not too close to you or your personal life, someone who can be objective). Even those of us who are a sounding board for others need someone who will listen when dealing with our own "stuff". Sometimes you can't see the forest for the trees, and you just need an outside perspective to keep things moving forward. I strongly encourage connecting with a coach or accountability partner to walk beside you on this journey.

I would love to be your personal coach and to support you as you transition from being fearful and powerless to becoming free and empowered. Please take a moment to watch the video where I explain what I offer, and sign up for a complimentary consultation call, if what I provide meets your needs. You can find the video at www.KENYARANSEY.com/iwantchange

About the Author

Kenya Ransey is an author-educator and lifestyle design coach for people who want to experience change for the better.

Standing in the Power of Being Alone has equipped Kenya to be her best self and to live her best life, which includes reading, writing, learning, spending time with family, connecting with others, and traveling extensively.

Visit KenyaRansey.com for more about Kenya and the work she does. (**Note the spelling of the last name**).

To learn more about working with Kenya directly, please refer to the section of this book titled "Next Steps", or visit www.KenyaRansey.com/iwantchange.

Acknowledgments

First and foremost, I thank God. The Spirit who leads, guides, and walks with me as I travel through this journey we call life. Apart from You, I am and can do nothing. (The Gospel According to John 15:5).

I also want to thank:

My father, James Leroy Ransey: Daddy, I did it! Thank you for always, always encouraging me and for telling me time and time again to "Shine bright. Be YOU, and don't change who you are because someone may be uncomfortable with your presence and what you represent." I miss you tremendously, Dad.

My mother, Jimalene (Jean): In so many ways, you are such a stellar example for everyone around you. I am eternally grateful that our multi-faceted relationship has allowed me to know you as mother, fellow woman, and friend. Love you, Ma.

My brother Jim: You were the very first person to tell me that what I have to say "other people need to hear". Thank you. You are a man of wisdom, and I hope you know how valuable you are to me.

My brother Jamie (Jame): Thank you for always supporting me by listening and providing guidance. I love you dearly.

My uncle, Harold Lindsey, Jr. (Unk): You planted a seed when you encouraged me to become a published author... many, many years ago. Thank you for your encouragement, support, and efforts to help me succeed.

My writing coach, Drew Rozell: Thank you for helping me to manifest what was merely a desire and a dream for far too long. You have helped unleash me onto the world, and for that I am grateful. Thank you, thank you, thank you!

My editor and fellow educator, Ann Downs: Thank you for partnering with me along this journey and for helping me be clearer and more concise in my writing. I believe our working together is the beginning of something uniquely special, and I appreciate you.

To Daliborka Mijailovic, my cover designer: I appreciate your gift. Thank you.

To each and every reader: I do not take it lightly that you trust me enough to allow me to share in your journey and to speak honestly from my heart and mind, to yours. It is the highest honor. Thank you!

Lastly, to those who were a tremendous help and service to me that were not listed here...please, please know it was not an intentional oversight of your invaluable contribution. I appreciate you and truly thank you for your service unto me.

With the utmost sincerity,

Kenya M. Ransey